Peter —

Thanks for
the Vote of
Confidence

The Canoe Theory

"The Secret Power of Cooperation"

Lessons to Successfully Navigate Through Corporate Waters

David R. Hibbard
Marhnelle S. Hibbard
John W. Stockman, Ph.D.

Editor: Tim Spurlock
Production Manager: Christina
Production Coordinator: Brian M. Steele
Marketing Coordinator: Sara Hinckley

Thomson Learning Custom Publishing
5191 Natorp Blvd.
Mason, Ohio 45040
USA

For information about our products, contact us:
1-800-355-9983
http://www.custom.thomsonlearning.com

International Headquarters
Thomson Learning
International Division
290 Harbor Drive, 2nd Floor
Stamford, CT 06902-7477
USA

UK/Europe/Middle East/South Africa
Thomson Learning
Berkshire House
168-173 High Holborn
London WCIV 7AA

Asia
Thomson Learning
60 Albert Street, #15-01
Albert Complex
Singapore 189969

Canada
Nelson Thomson Learning
1120 Birchmount Road
Toronto, Ontario MIK 5G4
Canada
United Kingdom

Visit us at www.e-riginality.com and learn more about this book and other titles published by Thomson Learning Custom Publishing

ISBN 0-759-30557-9

The Adaptable Courseware Program consists of products and additions to existing Custom Publishing products that are produced from camera-ready copy. Peer review, class testing, and accuracy are primarily the responsibility of the author(s).

THE CANOE THEORY

Which Canoe Best Suits You?

THE CANOE THEORY

IMAGINE YOUR COMPANY IS LIKE A LONG CANOE

THE COMPANY HAS A DIRECTION - A DESTINATION

EVERYONE HAS A SEAT AND A PADDLE AND EVERYONE
IS EXPECTED TO PADDLE

THOSE WHO WON'T PADDLE...
HAVE TO GET OUT OF THE CANOE

THOSE WHO PADDLE WELL, BUT PREVENT OTHERS FROM
PADDLING HAVE TO ADJUST OR GET OUT OF THE CANOE

THE CANOE THEORY BELIEVES IN BEING UNDERSTANDING
IF YOU HAVE A PERSONAL CRISIS YOUR COMPATRIOTS
WILL PADDLE FOR YOU FOR A REASONABLE PERIOD OF
TIME, TO GIVE YOU TIME TO ADJUST

THE CANOE THEORY SAYS YOU HAVE THE RIGHT TO BE
HAPPY. IF THERE IS *ANYTHING* YOU DON'T LIKE ABOUT
THE CANOE, THE CANOE WILL PULL OVER & ALLOW YOU
TO GET INTO A CANOE YOU LIKE

THE MORAL OF THE CANOE THEORY IS:

IF YOU ARE GOING TO BE IN THE CANOE THEN SUPPORT
THE CANOE OR HAVE THE INTEGRITY TO LEAVE, RATHER
THAN STAY AND UNDERMINE THE CANOE

CONTENTS

CONTENTS (continued)

Dedication...

To the individuals who shared their personal stories to make this possible, to the success of every individual making the right employment choice, and to the organizations standing for the best interests of the whole.

Foreword...

Following a 12-year corporate research study of employees and leaders in multiple corporations throughout the United States, Profit Techniques discovered astounding information. Research results indicated that approximately 87% of the corporations surveyed exhibited a disconnect between the organization's leadership and the employee.[1]

Generally speaking, few employees had a clear understanding of the direction, the core values, or the urgent initiatives of the company.

In most cases, when the research information was provided to the leaders of the corporation being researched, they were often shocked with the results expressed by the employee rank and file. Most leaders were certain that they had communicated where the organization was going, and what the key initiatives were to the employees. Not the case, not even close. The fact was, management was heading due North while employees were heading due South. The only one's that realized the truth were the employees!

In today's rapidly changing, complex world, every organization needs to communicate a basic philosophy of core beliefs, which shape and govern individual and collective behavior. This is commonly referred to as the organization's culture. Such a belief system identifies, for members of the organization, the behaviors necessary to reach individual and enterprise potential.

The Canoe Theory is a simple, yet powerful set of principles which, when properly implemented, form the foundation of a

---

[1] *Profit Techniques Leadership Research Study, 1989/2001.*

high-performance organization.

Based on many years of experience and multiple examples of organizational ineffectiveness, The Canoe Theory has been implemented in a multitude of organizations with profound results.

We believe that an organization's success is built on the dual concepts of individual excellence and collective achievement. The synergistic consequences of the interaction of these concepts are based upon three distinct factors, namely, *a positive attitude, a shared vision, and a commitment to team.*

In order for success to occur, every employee is expected to continuously ensure that his or her mix of behavior, attitude, skill and experience adds value to the overall organization's mission.

Everyone is responsible for his or her own employability: longevity and loyalty are not sufficient to guarantee job security.

In return, each organization must be committed to offering challenging work, a supportive work culture, opportunities for growth, and a reward system that inspires performance.

The Canoe Theory offers a depiction of a metaphor for a contemporary organizational philosophy designed for the 21st Century.

The names of individual organizations have been changed to protect confidentiality.

What follows are examples of The Canoe Theory's application and the behaviors necessary to maximize performance and results in any organization.

Note from the Authors...

These are reasons why others have implemented The Canoe Theory ... all with amazing success. If you experience any of the following, you most likely would benefit from the philosophy of the Canoe Theory.

> *If your company is in a growth mode*
> *If your company is losing market share*
> *If your company is stagnant*
> *If your company is reorganizing*
> *If your company is downsizing*
> *If your company is not satisfied with revenue*
> *If your company has a vision of achievement*

One last thought, you don't have to own the company to create change or to have your vision become a reality.

The following are a few examples of real companies and their implementation of The Canoe Theory.

David R. Hibbard
Marhnelle S. Hibbard
John W. Stockman, Ph.D.

A CASE STUDY

Company "A"

In 2001, the president of a Real Estate Property Management Group realized there was a "disconnect" between the Employees and Management.

This specific organization was "best in class" according to the following outside indicators: growth, profitability and acknowledgement from industry peers.

The president had a *dream* — a dream that if his organization were truly connected and truly focused on supporting one another as a team, they would fly!

Their customers would benefit and the people would love working there. There would be less attrition, they would attract top talent and the profits would be greater.

He was committed to making a difference in his people's lives, and since he employed over 650 individuals this would represent a significant feat.

Management developed several internal groups to focus on key issues, such as communication, appreciation of the people, and so on. But after a year, the president came to terms with the reality that they were not breaking through to the *real stuff*, the real issues.

On the surface it seemed that they were making progress.

However, the president found destructive conversations were being engaged behind the scenes.

Resolution

The president was determined to see his dream become a reality for the company.

He knew he needed support in shifting the organization, but didn't realize it had to start with him. He called on someone he respected for coaching.

That first conversation revolved around his natural leadership style within the company. The president found that in order for results to be different... it started with him.

He would need to shift first. The president took on the personal challenge and made a choice that forever shifted the destination of his company and his own commitment to his dream.

For months there were meetings on how to motivate everyone and keep them in the "canoe." The goal was to rally everyone into this new culture of people serving people!

Two and a half months into this process, the president brought together his entire organization and he and his management team rolled out the new vision.

There was a translator supporting the communication to ensure that everyone from maintenance manager to day porter to leasing consultant ... everyone, understood the new direction.

Ultimately, the president and his management team grew stronger each day and understood the need to support and coach their other teammates while holding them accountable to the new standards.

Today, this organization is living by the tenets of The Canoe Theory ... and, as they grow and continue to work through their issues, they stand for each other with honesty, with accountability and with open dialogue.

Their mantra is *"People Serving People."*

This organization was recently named one of the best places to work according to a national business journal publication.

During the economic shift of 2001, Company A responded with urgency, as a united front, and minimized the effects of market conditions.

The results were incredible.

- Personal performance went up

- Attrition went down by 40%

- All industry indicators (occupancy, rents, etc.) are at the top of the market

They are a living example of The Canoe Theory at work, now with 775 individuals working (paddling) together!

Company "B"

In San Francisco, California, two companies merged, creating more of a collision than a merger. One company was very *process* driven and one company was very *sales* driven.

That, in itself, created a challenge. However, the two new owners were fairly adept in handling people issues and communicating with one another.

They had made a commitment to the basic premise of The Canoe Theory.

They began bridging the gaps and joining the team with monthly general meetings and weekly communications, while beginning to establish a new culture.

The challenges seemed to be less each day while business really began to take off. New customers and existing customers were comfortable with the merger.

Everything seemed to be going in the right direction.

Company B was at maximum capacity with the existing staff. Everyone was working 60-hour weeks in order to keep up with the pace of the business. They were frantically looking for new talent to support the team.

Everyone was under tremendous pressure when management began to hear more and more of the power down methods of one division leader.

Then, the bottom fell out. The division leader, *Mark*, was out of control. He was abusing his power, belittling his people by yelling, demanding, and demoralizing anyone that came into his domain.

In the beginning, the owners rationalized his behavior due to his productivity and performance. He was the best in the industry and the clients loved him.

Resolution

The owners felt backed into a corner. They also believed they were acting out of integrity based on the principals of The Canoe Theory, specifically tenet five ...

> *"Those Who Paddle Well but Prevent Others from Paddling Have to Adjust or Get Out of the Canoe."*

The key leaders had numerous coaching conversations with *Mark* suggesting he adapt his behavior to support his team.

He replied that it was his way or the highway. He wasn't willing to adjust his leadership style or attitude.

As a result, *Mark* was released. It was a difficult thing to do since he was considered the industry's best, but never-the-less, management believed a commitment to The Canoe Theory was the foundation of their future.

A new succeeding division leader was promoted from within the department. It was soon discovered that the damage *Mark* had done was more significant than originally believed.

Mark had been the role model for his department and after a few weeks, leadership discovered that the new division leader had formed the same destructive habits as *Mark* and was also asked to resign.

It was soon realized that the poison had gone three tiers deep. *Mark*, the succeeding division leader, and the following leader in the succession line all had the same disparaging style.

Once everyone in the organization understood that performance and <u>attitude</u> both needed to be present to remain employed, the organization flourished.

The new leader within the troubled division mended the emotions of his division.

Standing for the respect of everyone is a key component of The Canoe Theory principles.

The entire organization experienced the value of The Canoe Theory.

It is extremely important to realize that "culture" defines the style and approach most people have while doing "business."
—Profit Techniques

PART **ONE**

THE CANOE THEORY: A TRUE STORY

"A vision."

THE CANOE THEORY: A TRUE STORY

It was a rainy, overcast day in early March of 1996 when Jeff Allen, the Owner and CEO of Glassco Production Industries, first began to think about the future of his organization.

He had been involved with Glassco in many capacities since 1986. Jeff never realized he would get into the equipment manufacturing industry; he was initially hired in sales.

Jeff worked his way from New Business Development Rep to Sales Manager to President/General Manager.

Finally, in 1995, Jeff purchased the business from several partners and became the sole owner.

Glassco had its share of success as well as times of challenge. There were times when new engineering projects in San Francisco, Washington, and Hawaii created very profitable results, but there were also economic downturns when sales were low and pay-cuts and lay-offs were the order of the day.

Overall, GPI had a very successful history and its reputation and image were extremely positive.

The firm gained notoriety for innovative engineering design work and manufacturing practices were seen by almost everyone as the best in the industry.

It was not the past that occupied Jeff's thoughts of today, but rather the future. He had begun to think about an exit strategy for himself and how that would play out for the future of Glassco.

He had spent considerable time contemplating what he wanted after spending ten years of his life building this organization.

The most obvious option seemed to be to sell the organization. Jeff had decided years before not to go through the uncertainties, difficulties and expenses of an IPO.

That would mean finding an outside party who could purchase the assets and goodwill. But would they understand the spirit of the firm he had worked so hard to create?

Over the previous years, Jeff had assembled a work group of over 75 industrial engineers and customer support and sales professionals many of which were extremely competent, committed, and loyal to him and to the business of GPI.

Many had been with him since he started with Glassco. His concern was that the new owners might not retain this talented group of people and might dismantle what he had worked so hard to create.

Jeff was concerned for his people and the success of the organization he had built.

At a recent conference he had attended, one of the speakers

advanced the model of an Employee Stock Ownership Plan (ESOP) as a strategy for transferring ownership of an organization.

The essence of an ESOP is that the employees purchase the firm from the owner and in turn become the owners themselves.

The concept had a great deal of appeal for Jeff and he decided to explore the details.

After six months of meetings with accountants, tax specialists, and attorneys, Jeff concluded that pursing an ESOP would best suit his goals and the future of GPI.

The employees would own the company in just five years and Jeff would be free to pursue other ventures.

There was just one minor challenge that Jeff had to conquer before he could truly have peace of mind about the future.

He had to have confidence that the management team that succeeded him would have the same level of commitment and sense of dedication that he had developed over the years.

This would not be easy, but he had time to develop a plan, through which he would pass on his legacy to Glassco employees.

Jeff spent many hours thinking about the foundation of Glassco, what its values were, what it stood for, and what led to its success.

He believed that if an organization combined individual excellence with collective achievement and if leadership maximized everyone's potential, they could then build an organization that would be envied by all.

An organization built on the dual concepts of individual excellence and collective achievements were key. This collective synergy would be based on three critical factors: *a positive attitude, a shared vision and a commitment to team.*

Jeff knew that each of these tenets had been a major factor behind Glassco's success, and that each must be carried forward by the employees.

Furthermore, he realized that in order to achieve success, every associate of GPI would be expected to continuously develop his or her mix of behavior, attitude, skill, and experience in order to add value to the mission of the organization.

He knew that each employee was responsible for his or her own employability; longevity and seniority would not guarantee future job security.

What Jeff knew above all was that GPI could offer each of the future owners the opportunity of a lifetime.

If they could continue to work together and reach the firm's potential, they would all enjoy economic rewards, gain market share, and partake in personal satisfactions beyond their wildest dreams.

He believed that if he could develop a philosophy, a "contract" so-to-speak, which captured the essence of Glassco and which could serve as a guide for all employees/owners to follow, he would create something that would forever influence the destiny of Glassco.

He also believed that such a philosophy could be applicable to any organization, private - public or non-profit, and could drive them to succeed as a high-performing enterprise.

All Jeff could think about for the next several weeks were the fundamental philosophies that he wanted to develop and instill in each Glassco associate.

Coincidentally, Jeff had recently returned from an industry conference where he had listened to a speaker share some concepts he felt were similar to those he wanted to create for GPI.

The concepts were expressed as a leadership principle called The Canoe Theory.

The thoughts and beliefs of The Canoe Theory pushed Jeff to begin mentally formulating a plan to implement what he had heard. He began by dissecting each tenet of The Canoe Theory and applying it to Glassco.

> *"I demand a commitment to excellence and to victory and that is what life is all about."*
> — *Vincent Lombardi*

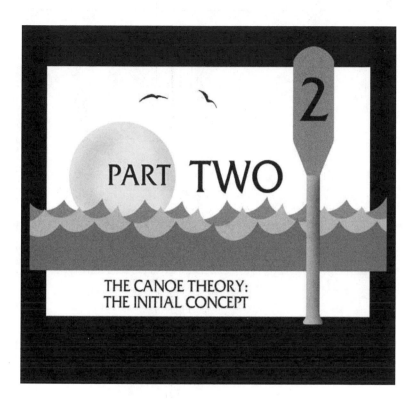

PART TWO

THE CANOE THEORY:
THE INITIAL CONCEPT

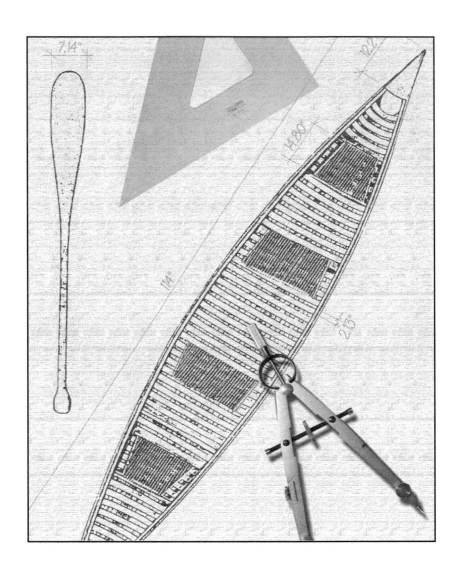

The Vision Needed A Blue Print,
i.e. a Plan.

THE INITIAL CANOE
THEORY CONCEPT

TENET #1
THINK OF YOUR COMPANY AS
A LONG CANOE

Jeff knew that for the future owners of Glassco Production Industries to succeed, they would all have to work together and see themselves in the same canoe.

There had been a culture that was established, one that truly defined the way GPI conducted business, brought in clients and supported their associates.

This culture was at the heart of what made Glassco different from its competitors.

Jeff also realized that without himself at the helm he questioned if others would understand the importance of maintaining these successful traditions.

These values and "rules of doing business" had been at the core of attracting top talent for Glassco.

This entrepreneurial culture had allowed GPI to be the leader in their field and stay at the forefront of their industry.

Jeff believed it was a fact that, to succeed, everyone had to be actively involved in the success of the organization's effort.

Each employee was to be responsible and accountable for his or her own performance and for the performance of others.

Jeff knew that inter-dependence among all employees was necessary to achieve overall goals.

GPI would not survive if, individually and collectively, everyone was not in the "canoe."

Jeff thought, what if everyone were on the same page and understood that actively working together was the key to success? Wow - what a powerful thought!

But, without direction, they would drift 'hither and yon' — with no destination.

He believed the overall organization must have a shared vision, which would provide a collective direction and purpose.

Jeff realized this was a key component to discovering the meaning of The Canoe Theory and at all costs he was committed to preserve the traditions in place and share this vision with everyone at Glassco.

He was ready for the second theme of The Canoe Theory:

"Bureaucracy strangles. Informality liberates. Creating an informal atmosphere is a competitive advantage."
                                                        —*Jack Welch*

TENET #2
THE CANOE HAS
A DESTINATION

What is more powerful than a shared vision, a future everyone can support and be enthused about?

Jeff thought if he could communicate to everyone a challenging, yet achievable vision for their future, they could get the canoe moving in an exciting direction.

He understood that everyone should have the opportunity to contribute his or her ideas and help in the development of the vision.

He also knew that his team was to understand and believe in the mission or core purpose of GPI in order to secure maximum commitment.

This meant communication at all levels and in all directions for a complete "buy in" was critical.

Goals, objectives, activities, and tasks would all flow from the mission and vision and would guide the canoe to an exciting future.

Jeff began to think about how he could achieve this shared vision.

He knew that it had to be created with more than his own ideas because the people who would inherit the vision would be around long after he was gone.

Every individual at Glassco had to embrace the same passion and commitment in order to create a future for the organization and themselves, and their ideas were critical to the crafting of the direction that GPI would follow.

Following the metaphor of Glassco as a long canoe with a direction, Jeff realized that, for the organization to be successful, everyone in the canoe had to have a place to operate from.

Hence, the third tenet was implemented:

"Few things are impossible to diligence and skill…Great works are performed not by strength, but perseverance."

—*Samuel Johnson*

TENET #3
EVERYONE IN THE CANOE HAS A SEAT, AND A PADDLE, AND EVERYONE IS EXPECTED TO PADDLE

The vision of Glassco would never be realized unless every associate fulfilled the expectations associated with their particular function.

It was not enough to just be in the canoe. Each and every person would have to clearly understand the roles they would play, the activities for which they would be responsible, and how they would be held accountable.

Roles and responsibilities are the "seats and paddles" of an organization.

If everyone were to flawlessly execute his or her duties, the canoe would move steadily forward.

Jeff made a mental note to connect compensation to this theme. It seemed logical that salaries, bonuses and commissions should be directly related to how well each associate achieved the expectations of his or her roles and responsibilities.

It was several days before Jeff moved forward in his own thought process of implementing The Canoe Theory. He seemed to be stuck on the third theme of roles and responsibilities.

The next thought emerged quite unexpectedly when Jeff arrived at GPI early one morning and found Irene, who was not one of GPI's best employees, surfing the web at her desk.

Jeff knew that Irene came in early to get out a rush order, but it was obvious that nothing productive was happening at her desk.

Bingo! Just what The Canoe Theory had preached . . . you can't just sit in the canoe, you have to paddle!

Later that day he thought more about Irene and realized that the vision of GPI would never be reached unless everyone paddled.

There was one manager Jeff knew that he could trust and rely on to always perform at the highest level, and that was Carol. She was in charge of technical design and had been an employee of GPI for a long time.

When he compared Irene to Carol it was like comparing night and day.

Jeff spent more time and energy "managing" Irene than he did mentoring Carol, and it didn't seem right. If everyone were like Carol, in skills, attitude and behavior, the canoe would glide even more effectively towards its goals.

He realized he needed to make adjustments with his expectations of Irene and others. He made a note in his book:

$$A + P = E$$

Attitude + Performance = Employability

—Profit Techniques

TENET #4
THOSE WHO WON'T PADDLE
HAVE TO GET OUT
OF THE CANOE

A few weeks passed before Jeff could solidify his thoughts around this principle.

Jeff drew upon the examples within his own sales division where he had senior sales professionals whose performance had dropped off from the early years.

These individuals at one time were top players in the game. They began to lose key accounts due to market conditions and the tenacity needed to bring on new accounts was non-existent.

When management would question the reports or lack of business, the sales reps would tell their story of why business wasn't happening.

These well-articulated excuses began to add up. Jeff remembered that for the reps to remain employed, loyalty wasn't the only deciding factor.

They would have to create results to stay in the canoe.

Outside of the sales division, it would also be imperative that each person in the canoe create the results that they were hired to create, no matter what division.

Coordination, cooperation and collaboration would have to be key principles in all divisions of the organization.

Jeff grabbed his book once more and wrote a reminder to himself, "If they don't paddle they have to get out of the canoe."

Excuses won't make it anymore. This statement was to be a core element to the success of GPI.

As he reflected on the past highs and lows, Jeff thought of the next premise of this leadership process:

$$L + AWAE = E$$
Loyalty + A Well-Articulated Excuse ≠ Employment
—*Profit Techniques*

TENET #5
THOSE WHO PADDLE WELL,
BUT PREVENT OTHERS FROM
PADDLING,
HAVE TO ADJUST
OR GET OUT OF THE CANOE

Finally, The Canoe Theory was beginning to come together for Jeff.

He knew that the ultimate success of Glassco was hidden in the ability of everyone in the organization to pull together, to blend their diverse talents and to work as a team.

He also knew that the attitude each of the associates displayed through their behavior was the real key to long term growth and achievement.

Jeff realized that no single individual should be allowed to hamper the destination of the canoe.

He knew that the whole is as important as the part.

He understood that some of the employees were exceptional performers and as a result, they were important to the production of the organization.

Jeff also understood that even though certain individuals performed exceptionally well, there could be no exceptions for Prima Donna performers.

An example of that was Rick, he was an exceptional Installation and Services Manager, but he was always late for meetings, holding up staff.

In fact, half of the time, Rick wouldn't return his colleagues' phone calls for days. He definitely was not supporting others.

Jeff understood that in order for Glassco to reach the apex of success, everyone would be required to maintain a supportive attitude for the team.

Once again, he thought, "The whole must not suffer because of the part."

Realistically, Jeff knew that as economic markets shift, and personnel issues arose, GPI would face unforeseen crises in the future— both individually and organizationally.

He knew changes would occur that would cause Glassco to alter course or adopt new strategies. And, the reality of imminent change would cause stress and anxiety for everyone.

As much as Jeff didn't like to think about such things, he needed to have the organization and all individuals involved support the understanding, philosophy, and approach to deal with such realities. And the sixth tenet came to life for Jeff:

"One man can be a crucial ingredient on a team, but one man cannot make a team."

— *Kareem Abdul-Jabbar, NBA Center*

TENET #6
THE CANOE THEORY
IS UNDERSTANDING

Valued associates who experience stress or personal crisis that hinders their potential must be nurtured and supported by the organization with appropriate intervention strategies.

The reality of The Canoe Theory is based on TEAM (Together Everyone Achieves More), which includes assisting associates when a personal crisis presents itself.

Jeff acknowledged that GPI would face crises in the coming years and that everyone would be tested by their ability to pull together to meet those challenges.

Everyone needed to understand how to support a colleague in need. This was at the core of GPI's culture.

Each individual needed to know that if they faced a significant crisis in their life, they could, for a reasonable amount of time, put down their paddle and their team would pick up the slack.

This was a critical point of building a sustainable organization. People serving and supporting each other.

Jeff realized the rate of change in the business world was relentless. Pressure was going to be part of the daily climate of business.

This seemed to apply as far into the future as Jeff could see. Every associate must be in the canoe together working to reach a common destination. Anything less would not be acceptable short of a personal crisis.

Jeff believed that personal crisis was inevitable just as corporate difficulties were. He understood that personal crisis would be best supported by each individual's effort to "take up the slack" when a member needed support.

Jeff knew that the organization he envisioned for his associates would be dedicated to the success of each individual that was in the GPI canoe!

That meant everyone who chose to be in the canoe would be supported provided that they perform on a superior level everyday.

If an employee began acting out, not playing team ball, not supporting the canoe in the manner dedicated by the philosophy of The Canoe Theory, they would be putting themselves and their employability at risk.

Jeff focused on the final and most powerful point:

"The ultimate measure of a man is not where he stands in moments of comfort and convenience, but where he stands at times of challenge and controversy."

— *Martin Luther King, Jr.*

TENET #7
THE CANOE THEORY SAYS YOU HAVE A RIGHT TO BE HAPPY

A powerful release of energy came over Jeff. He thought, if any individual put him or herself at risk in the canoe... they just couldn't be happy.

It made so much sense to Jeff that a happy employee would never participate in self-sabotage or essentially put themselves at risk.

Jeff was puzzled at the thought that an individual who had the ability to paddle well, wouldn't!

Additionally, why anyone would interfere with others, be uncooperative or under-perform, and essentially sabotage their employment future?

He decided that the final concept of The Canoe Theory was in support of all the employees...everyone has a right to be happy.

Perhaps they didn't like where the canoe was going or who was in the canoe, or where they were sitting, or didn't like the paddle they had... whatever.

The canoe would simply pull over to shore and let the employee off so they could get in a canoe that they did like!

And there are so many canoes, so many destinations, so many cultures, and so many choices, why would an individual be in a canoe that made them unhappy?

Jeff realized that because an employee was not happy, or discovered that they were in a canoe that didn't fit their interests, it shouldn't create a negative response with the leaders of the organization.

The leaders simply needed to understand that if they really cared about every single individual, they would support that person in leaving the canoe so they could ultimately be happy. Simple!

At last, Jeff understood the simplicity and complexity of The Canoe Theory philosophy.

He had articulated it in his mind and personalized it with his vision and was ready to integrate it into GPI. He knew he was now ready to move forward.

The first step would be to have a meeting with all of the employees to communicate the direction of the canoe, requesting each individual contemplate if this was the canoe for them.

He was spirited with the thought of the growth and potential for Glassco and each individual that chose "in."

He had the basic components of a successful organization stated in a simple, understandable set of tenets... The Canoe Theory.

The challenge ahead was to implement these leadership principles across the culture of GPI. It was a challenge, but Jeff knew the results would be rewarding for all.

POSTSCRIPT

On December 31, 2001, Jeff's dream became a reality and Glassco became one of the few wholly employee owned ESOP's in the United States.

"There are two ways of spreading light, to be the candle or the mirror that reflects it."

— *Edith Warton*

PART THREE

THE CANOE THEORY:
A PRACTICAL APPLICATION

The blue print materialized into a reality.

TENET #1
THE COMPANY IS LIKE
A LONG CANOE

The Canoe Theory theme establishes the fact that everyone is directly involved in the success of the organization.

A more common notion is "we're all in the same canoe" and thus responsible and accountable for our own and each other's performance.

We are inextricably dependent upon one another for success and we cannot reach our potential if, individually or collectively, we are not all "in the canoe."

The culture of the canoe is created by core values, beliefs and the established "rules" of conduct. And, cultural differences distinguish organizations and competitors from one another.

The point being, there are tremendous cultural diversities and challenges among canoes.

When you begin building, rebuilding or refining towards an even more effective organization, you need a true perspective of how the culture is perceived. Remember perception is reality.

All canoes are uniquely structured... expectations differ, style differs and therefore culture differs.

Culture is extremely important to the success of the canoe. It defines the system of interactions within a specific group, team and canoe.

These systems of interactions are based upon acquired values, beliefs and rules of conduct. It is the foundation of what is acceptable and what isn't.

There are 3 key areas that speak volumes when referring to culture.

> *Environment*
> *Customers*
> *People*

We sometimes become oblivious to our environment or our philosophy of how we treat our customers or people within our canoe.

We walk by a coffee stained carpet or cluttered storage rooms; we ignore the look of our office, most importantly the reception area.

We often don't review corporate expectations with regards to answering the phones in terms of friendliness or how we specifically provide customer service.

Thoughts for the Leaders...

Stand back and take a fresh look at your existing culture starting with the environment.

Take a Sunday Walk-Through. On any "non-business" day walk through your facility and look around. What is the office communicating to you as you examine the view? You are encouraged to evaluate all areas from the mindset of an outsider.

Be objective, as if you had no connection to the organization... your canoe. Take in what you experience, become more aware.

General areas to focus on would be...

- Is your outside entrance and lobby inviting?

- Is it necessary that you operate with a locked security entrance?

- Is the reception area open or intimidating?

- Is the reception desk and areas behind the desk organized, clean, etc?

- Are the plants dead in the corner?

- How does each department lay out for communication?

- Does this represent a culture in which you are prideful?

- Is this the way you intended to represent your organization?

The next area of focus should be customer & people focused:

- Does someone greet everyone entering the lobby in a friendly manner?

- If the person entering the reception area is required to wait, are they offered a refreshment?

- How does it feel when you call into your office? Is the reception on the other end of the telephone warm and inviting?

- Ask yourself, would you want to do business with this company?

- Is the experience of doing business with your company (canoe) easy and enjoyable, or rigid?

- Is the organization client centric?

- Are the employees vested or just focused on their lunch hour?

- Does the organization meet your expectations?

Next, take the customer challenge! What do your clients perceive the culture to be?

- Have an executive from your firm take the time to have a sincere conversation with some of your key customers... get their perspective.

- Ask new employees what their perception of the organization was before being hired and after being hired.

- Ask a potential candidate that didn't take the job... why they didn't and what their perception of the canoe was.

- Ask vendors how they would rank your organization as it pertains to ease of doing business, competency and attitude.

- Hire an outside group to research existing clients or potential new clients.

- If you are in a professional group, ask a colleague to "shop" the organization.

- The "shopper" might be a prospective client calling in for pricing or asking for a proposal.

- Request feedback on his or her perception of the existing culture.

Note: It is critical that ALL research information be held confidential.

Thoughts for Associates...

The culture truly defines the essence of the organization — the canoe.

By joining or being in a canoe, you are buying into the canoe's beliefs.

- Confirm that your values and beliefs are in line with those of the canoe.

- You must be able to determine if the canoe's style represents a culture where you can personally succeed and at the same time make a solid contribution to the canoe.

- Evaluate if this is a platform where your skill set fits. It's up to you to ask yourself the question... "do I fit?"

The Bottom Line...

It's important to realize, that among all functional canoes, common denominators do exist.

Functional canoes rely on strong leadership and an overall sense of team.

Functional canoes have a clear purpose, course, culture and destination.

This purpose, course, culture and destination requires the successful coordination of all members of the canoe.

To do this, you must know what kind of canoe you are joining.

Do your best to understand the overall objective of the canoe, its style and identity — the culture.

Whatever your position, manager or associate, as you discover the environment/culture that exists ask yourself if it supports your values, beliefs and your passion.

Being in a canoe where there are mutually respected goals, values and beliefs will make the challenging times you will face ahead much easier.

Remember, no company or position you might hold is perfect and no company or position ever will be perfect.

Being challenged and finding yourself uncomfortable occasionally, is not the same as being in a position where a proper fit doesn't exist.

Challenges are a healthy and important component of your position.

When you breakthrough challenges within your organization, you not only are growing as an individual, but you are adding value to the canoe.

The limit to which you have accepted being comfortable is the limit to which you have grown.

TENET #2
THE CANOE HAS A DESTINATION

The organization must establish a vision that captures a future that all members can support. This desired state must be challenging, achievable and stimulating so that everyone in the canoe is motivated to reach this destination

.

A shared vision is one of the most powerful forces an organization can unleash on a daily basis. Ideally, there is an opportunity for everyone to input his or her ideas in the development of the vision.

In order for a canoe to most effectively serve its intended purpose, it needs to have a destination that is clearly defined.

Typically that destination is established at the top of the organization, but in some cases it is up to a division, a department or for that matter an individual to be the visionary.

The key point is, if there is no clear vision of where the canoe is going in your organization, your department or your group, you may be the individual that needs to step up and get involved by taking a lead.

Thoughts for the Leaders...

- Take responsibility for establishing a clear direction for your group.

- The destination of the canoe should be well defined and your employees should know how to support getting to this destination.

- Because you have the "Mission Statement" immortalized in granite in the lobby doesn't mean the employees know where the canoe is going.

Lets take a minute to define the word "destination" in a different way...

Imagine all of the personnel from the company are standing at the base of a mountain. At base camp the top executive says, "Our goal is to reach the summit. That will be the defining moment when we can say the organization has succeeded."

The top leader understands better than anyone that the climb will have moments when it will be extremely difficult. They know there will be times when things will go smoothly and times when everyone will be challenged.

When asked if they are up for the climb, most employees will say, "I'm in!" especially the new employees. The problem is, employees often "buy-in" without understanding that what lies ahead may be more challenging than what they bargained for.

The early part of the climb is not where the trouble is, it's further along on the climb where the going often gets especially difficult.

When times get tough, employees often complain, become negative, stop caring or even bail out.

What causes this disconnect? What keeps them from maintaining their original commitment to fight to the top of the summit as they initially said they would?

The answer is this; employees often lose interest because they end up feeling that they are not winning personally, they think it's some executive or owner, who are the big winners and as a result they ask, "Why should I?"

This attitude takes hold after the initial climb, and when times get tough. The question is, "what can leadership do about it"?

The best thing you can do is find out without making the employee uncomfortable, what's in it for them to pay the price....what is their win?

If you think it's money you may be right, or you may be wrong. It could be much deeper than that.

When you discover what personally motivates the employee to continue the climb you will have discovered the turbocharger that will keep them going through thick and thin.

- A key step for you as a leader is to care enough to ask your employees what they work for.

- What is it that they want from working at the organization

... in a deep sense?

- Certainly, employees should fight for the company dream, after all, that is what they committed to do when they joined the canoe, but shouldn't they also be committed to their own dream?

- Discover their personal dream; tell them that you see your role as a leader being one to support them in getting what they want.

- You can be assured that when you do this, with as many members of your team as possible, you will have found the secret to a new level of commitment from those who are making the climb with you. Remember, everyone has a dream.

Thoughts for Associates...

- Supporting the company destination is something that you will be required to become a part of.

- Through investigation, you will substantiality increase the probability of finding a canoe that represents a good fit... the right culture for you.

- When selecting a canoe, seek answers to these questions...

  - Where is the canoe going?

  - When and how does it plan to reach its destination?

  - Do the leaders and team members seem like individuals that you want to rely on, work and interact with?

  - Does your intuition say "yes"?

  - Does the canoe appear sturdy enough to stay afloat in rough waters or adverse conditions?

- Make sure that leaders understand where the canoe is going, and determine if they seem to have a clear view of how they will support the canoe.

- Ideally, the canoe's destination will support the realization of each member's personal objectives.

- By supporting the canoe's destination, you should also be able to reach your personal and professional goals as well.

- Make sure you take the time to understand what you want to achieve within this canoe.

- Since you will be expected to pay the price, you need to discover what you want personally and when. Ask yourself if the price you will be required to pay in this canoe will contribute to your personal dream.

- Remember, the organization has a right to expect your total commitment, just make sure your total commitment involves your personal dream as well.

- When you get to the top of the summit there should be two flags in the ground, one for the company and one for you.

The Bottom Line...

All canoes should have a clear and defined destination.

The destination is best accomplished if every member of the canoe is able to connect a personal win to the achievement of this destination, as well as support the organization's objective.

Segments of this journey may not always be smooth.

Clear and constant communication is critical to the success of the journey and must be at the top of the list.

Although leadership might post the destination, talk about it or meet about it, that doesn't mean everyone "gets it" – you need to ask!

Often individuals join a firm with vigor for the destination at the start only to lose faith during the tough parts of the climb. A sustained effort requires a "personal" connection with the destination.

TENET #3
EVERY MEMBER HAS A SEAT AND A PADDLE AND EVERYONE IS EXPECTED TO PADDLE

It is impossible for the canoe to reach its destination if everyone does not fulfill the expectations associated with participation.

Roles and responsibilities reflect seats and paddles and each must understand how the excellent execution of their duties moves the canoe forward.

Simply put, no one rides for minimal or no effort. You cannot sit on the side and "dangle your feet." ...This is a dynamic, constantly moving canoe.

Everyone must continually perform to the limits of their capabilities or they must be removed from the canoe. Poor performance is not an option in a functioning canoe.

To reach its destination with the greatest possible efficiency, the canoe must allocate and utilize its resources effectively.

To do this, all members must contribute to the canoe's progress.

This is best achieved when each member has a clear understanding of where he or she fits within the canoe and how he or she is expected to paddle.

It is equally important that members understand how their contribution supports the functions of other teammates within the canoe and ultimately how their function affects the overall progression of the canoe itself.

Functions will vary. No matter what his or her function is, every member has one. There can be no passive weight inside a well functioning canoe.

Whether it is a leader providing the canoe's direction or an employee providing inspiration, everyone can make a difference. Each individual's seat or position must support an efficient allocation of the canoe's resources – you must sit where you fit.

The seat where you are able to best serve the canoe may not be your first choice. Your individual function must support the overall direction of the canoe.

There are no "special seats" no "special paddles". This means that every contributing member of the canoe should be considered as important as any other.

Thoughts For Leaders...

- Leaders need to be able to identify a member's talent and place them in the canoe where their utility can be maximized.

- As a leader, what you want most is a team of individuals that will do whatever it takes to support the canoe, right?

- It shouldn't matter where they sit. If employees are vested in the company they will exhibit an attitude of "What can I do to help" rather than "it's not my job".

- One reason an employee can become negative, destructive, etc. may be due to the fact they don't feel vested in the direction of the canoe.

- Complainers on the team need to "snap out of it," get on board, and drop the petty complaining about where they sit or what's wrong with their paddle.

- A solid canoe of individuals, work with what they are given, or better said, they make it work!

- Avoid operating with the formula, L + AWAE = E. (Loyalty + A Well Articulated Excuse = Employment). Consider A + P = E (Attitude + Performance = Employment).

- However, if the organization simply does not have the resources to provide the ideal tools or situation at the moment, you need to explain the situation to the employee...

- Inform them that the tools they have are the best the organization can do at this given time.

- Remind them of the direction the company is taking and why it's important. Remind them "if we all pay the price in various ways" we all will win as a team and as individuals.

- If they continue to complain, consider the alternative of release. Let them get into a canoe they like.

- Always consider your Human Resource policies and procedures (make certain all conversations are documented and check legal resources).

Thoughts For Associates...

- Organizations don't always have the perfect tools that employees desire; sometimes the seat and paddle won't be optimum – that may be how it has to be for the time being.

- No matter what, you are expected to paddle. If for some reason you don't paddle or won't paddle you will be asked to leave the canoe.

- When you join the canoe, you make a commitment to act in accordance to the rules of the canoe. One key rule of all canoes is "you have to paddle."

- If you discover you have made a mistake in joining the canoe, you will still be required to paddle until you decide to find a different canoe.

- You may want to examine why you are unwilling to paddle. The odds are it may be more about you than the canoe. Take a look at your contribution to the issue before you make decisions that the canoe is in error.

The Bottom Line...

As a leader, you should cross train your team in critical areas in order to gain a base line of knowledge for each member's position.

In doing this, leaders will be able to create a more functional and efficient team and further identify and develop the breadth of talent that each team member possesses.

Leaders need to understand what motivates the individuals on their team and then place them accordingly within the organization.

Employees must be honest with themselves and with their teams.

If an employee knows that they do not fit, it is their responsibility to do something about it.

TENET #4
THOSE WHO WON'T PADDLE HAVE TO GET OUT OF THE CANOE

Everyone is required to paddle on a continual basis, there is not sufficient room in the canoe for an individual to just "sit, and not paddle."

This notion underscores the importance of a positive attitude and a commitment to action.

Effective canoes support the weight of all members, as they move towards their overall destination, but remember, no " passive weight" is allowed.

Given this, those who will not or cannot paddle must get out of the canoe.

A strong canoe will not tolerate the negative affects any member generates.

Those who will not paddle drain potential and morale of the whole and in the long run destroy their own potential as well.

In a dysfunctional canoe, those who won't paddle can hide, sometimes for years! Functional canoes discover the "non-paddlers" quickly and take action.

Thoughts For Leaders...

- Evaluate who is in the canoe... listen; look for signals of low production. Is the low production due to individuals not paddling?

- Once discovered, act on those not paddling... make decisions relative to the employee on the basis of A + P= E (Attitude + Performance = Employment).

- Removing a member of the canoe that will not paddle will support the whole and more importantly the individual that will not paddle.

- Train your managers on what signals to look for to identify "non paddlers"... understand that acting on non-paddlers will yield a resurgence of respect for management.

- By protecting the stability of the canoe through making the tough decisions, the organization prospers.

- Stand for the employee by having the courage to let them move on. (Always seek legal advice and counsel your managers on proper conduct when dealing with measurement of employees and termination issues).

Thoughts For Associates...

- It is your responsibility as an employee to understand what constitutes the standards of acceptable paddling (performance).

- You must do whatever is necessary within legal, moral, and ethical boundaries to achieve the benchmark that management has provided.

- Realize that the higher in stature you may be the more you become an extension of leadership.

- As a top performer, you will be expected to support leadership, attend meetings, be positive and contribute to the canoe as a professional.

- Participating in gossip or negative talk within the ranks is unacceptable.

- Despite any perceived leadership issues you may have, as long as you are a part of the canoe, you have an obligation to support the canoe.

The Bottom Line...

There is no "passive weight" allowed in the canoe. That is, all weight in the canoe must serve a purpose and support the canoe in its endeavor.

There must be standards set in place defining what is acceptable and unacceptable behavior.

Realize that no single individual wants to sit in a canoe and look across to another paddler and say to themselves, why is this person in this canoe? Competent employees expect competency around them.

Employees want to be surrounded by people who inspire, who motivate, who have good energy, who are team players, who contribute, who are kind, who are ethical and who pull their load.

Paddling can be defined as reaching the benchmarks that are set. If you don't or won't even attempt to reach them you should expect removal from the canoe.

The canoe will not reach its destination with mediocre, sub-standard performance. The definition of what "paddling" is must be clearly defined. Once again, communication is key.

TENET #5
THOSE WHO PADDLE WELL BUT PREVENT OTHERS FROM PADDLING MUST ADJUST OR GET OUT OF THE CANOE

Reaching a destination depends upon the coordinated efforts of everyone.

The canoe moves smoothly and surely toward its destination when synchronization and coordination are achieved.

Synergy is reached when people act in unison as a team to achieve a shared vision.

Those who are not team players, those who do not paddle, must get out of the canoe.

The most dangerous individual in the canoe is one that is negative or interferes with the positive performance of others.

If these individuals will not adjust, they must be removed from the canoe. Once again, A + P = E (Attitude + Performance = Employment).

No one individual should be exempt from the standards established for the canoe, no matter what their revenue performance indicates.

Thoughts For Leaders...

- Often, a great performer will produce exceptionally well and will interact positively with management, but subsequently interacts with other employees negatively! It's a kind of "kiss up", "power down" scenario. Essentially, they are friendly and cooperative with management and rude to subordinates or fellow workers.

- Management may be unaware of the destructive nature of these individuals since they are often blinded by the individual's high performance.

- Avoid the poor choice of choosing to look the other way!

- Leadership's responsibility is to the team – the whole.

- Leaders cannot afford to make concessions to a "hot-shot" in the canoe if the style of this person's performance is adversely impacting the performance of others. **No exceptions.**

- Leaders must not allow themselves to become "hostage" to top performers. Doing so will soon mean the "tail wags the dog."

- As a leader, it's a mistake to think that a person's productivity out-weighs the adversity they create within the canoe.

- *"Hot Shots"* or *"Prima Donnas"* must be controlled or removed from the canoe if they are destructive to the whole.

- Meeting or surpassing a goal individually, but not participating as a team member is not acceptable, this should be considered not paddling.

- Listen to the mass employee opinions and the volume of those opinions and you may discover who in the canoe is missing the "A" for attitude in A + P = E.

Thoughts For Associates...

- Your contribution must be made in a positive manner. Negativity is unacceptable.

- Consider the fact that along the way someone assisted you when you were an average paddler.

- Now that you have done well, don't lose your humility.

- Realize that to be a "pro" means total cooperation. You will be admired and held high when you come from a place of achievement and cooperation. Not achievement and "attitude."

- Provide a positive professional perspective and be willing to confront those who participate negatively in the canoe.

- You have a responsibility to address the negative situation in the canoe and attempt to create a positive change.

- If change is not implemented, you have a choice: leave the canoe for one that makes you happy or remain supportive.

- If you are a positive paddler, and you take your frustration to the top regarding a negative paddler and don't get what you want you need to exercise the right choice: Either leave the canoe or stay and support it by not gossiping about the poor results you feel you got.

- Spreading negativity is not the solution, and you will ultimately undermine the canoe and your own personal integrity.

The Bottom Line...

If you hate the canoe you are in you should consider getting into a canoe you like.

Being a great paddler with outstanding results is only being half a professional. The other half is acting like one.

Realize that no one is indispensable.

Be respected for $A + P = E$.

Wake up to the fact that humility often comes when you fall from your perch. If you are in sales, remember, your productivity may change... all oil wells dry up!

As a leader take a brave stand, realize that attitude is a key component for the canoe's success!

TENET #6
THE CANOE UNDERSTANDS CRISIS

The canoe theory understands crisis.

If a member of the canoe has a death in the family, an illness, a health issue or any personal crisis, the canoe will pull over to shore and allow the individual to solve their crisis for a reasonable period of time, while the other team members take up the paddling.

Personal lives and business lives are entwined; one affects the other.

If an individual is experiencing a crisis or great personal difficulty, they need to consider sharing the situation with their superiors in order to obtain understanding for what may be poor paddling due to crisis.

In most cases a reasonable time away from the organization may support the member and resolve the issue.

Compassion is a great leadership virtue.

Everyone at one time or another runs into personal crisis in the canoe.

Leaders should choose to express compassion.

Nothing builds respect for management more than an extension of compassion in a period of employee crisis.

Consider crisis to be anything that will completely take an employee's mind off of the job at hand - paddling. Such as...

- Death in Family or Near the Family Circle

- Alcohol or Drug Correction (Consider your policy, procedures manual, to coincide with Federal and State Law)

- Emotional Crisis

- Physical Injury

- Financial crisis

- Nature's Destruction: Flood, Earthquake, Etc.

Listen with compassion, probe as deep as Human Resources would allow and as the employee feels comfortable sharing.

Thoughts For Leaders...

- As a leader you are required to foster an environment of trust and confidentiality among the team.

- You must be in tune with your employees so that they are able to recognize when an individual is having a problem.

- Let the team know, in a general and confidential manner, that a team member is experiencing personal difficulty and that they should expect less from this person for a short period of time. (See HR before you share, even if the employee approves).

- This sharing helps to hedge against speculation, rumors, and resentment in the canoe.

- When "helping" the troubled employee, leaders should be clear that they are not acting in a manner that will result in employee litigation.

- Human Resources should always be consulted.

- Agree upon a reasonable period of time for correction. Remind them that their compatriots will take up the paddling.

Thoughts For Associates...

- As an employee you need to let management know if something is beginning to influence your performance in the canoe.

- You should seek outside help when the crisis presents itself or discuss your crisis with the organization's HR department.

- You are accountable to have a plan for recovery when you experience crisis.

- It is your responsibility to recover within a reasonable period of time as established by mutual agreement with management.

The Bottom Line...

Every canoe will experience members who face unexpected crisis.

The best canoes are those with a foundation of understanding and cooperation.

Canoes with members who share the core value of teamwork will always take up the slack for those in crisis.

Temporary release from the canoe should be in line with HR and legal guidelines.

Compassion builds powerful canoes.

Employees in turn must realize that organizations also experience crisis.

As a result, the employee must exhibit understanding and allow the canoe to take time to re-group.

This will require the employee to "take up the slack" for the canoe until it has time to resolve its crisis.

TENET #7
THE CANOE SAYS YOU HAVE A RIGHT TO BE HAPPY

The Canoe Theory states that everyone has a fundamental right to be happy. Why should anyone want to stay in a canoe in which they are not happy?

The Canoe Theory holds that if an individual member in the canoe is not happy for any reason, the canoe will simply pull over to shore and let that individual out so they can get into a canoe they like.

This means if the member doesn't like the paddle, where they sit, where the canoe is going, who leads the canoe or anything at all, they have a right to leave and find a canoe that better suits them.

Life is too short to be involved in a canoe you cannot get behind. Everyone in an organization must realize that being in any canoe is a choice.

Thoughts For Leaders...

- As the leader of your canoe you need to be in touch with your people. You need to be able to identify the "temperature" of the canoe and the individuals in it.

- You should recognize and monitor the contribution of members on the team.

- Changes in an individual's contribution may reflect a strong indication of their happiness.

- If an individual is not happy, it may not always be about the canoe, they may need to look at themselves.

- You need to be a good listener. Leading your canoe requires compassion; if an individual's not happy in the canoe, it generally will show in attitude, performance, or both!

- If the employee isn't happy and you as the leader feel you have done all that is possible, it may be time to assist the individual with the option of seeking another canoe.

- Termination is often a gift and gives new opportunity to the employee.

Thoughts For Associates...

- As a member of the canoe you need to monitor your own behavior. Ask yourself, "Am I happy?"

- Don't be a victim... the power is yours.

- If you are not happy with the canoe you are in for any reason, find one where you can be happy, or build your own.

- Realize that if you are not happy, there is always a canoe where you can find a great fit.

- It is your responsibility to have the courage to find a canoe that's just right for you.

- Staying in a canoe that is not a "fit" only leads to frustration, resentment and poor performance... the end result is often termination.

- Be open to the possibility that staying in a canoe where you are unhappy is more painful than having the courage to seek out a new one.

- If you decide to stay in the canoe, despite the fact that you are unhappy, you need to have the integrity to support leadership and the canoe.

- Gossip, negativity, passive aggressive behavior, loss of interest etc; demonstrates little integrity.

Make the choice to get "in" or look for a canoe you prefer.

The Bottom Line...

No one should be in a canoe they are unhappy with.

Being in a canoe that represents a wrong fit leads to underperformance, frustration and ultimately, a negative attitude.

Staying in a canoe that is wrong for the individual is a matter of choice. You need to take full accountability for continuing that choice.

When you come from the position that you would like to leave the canoe, but can't for some reason, then you need to have the integrity to maintain a positive attitude and paddle with 100% effort until you can get into a canoe you like.

It's everyone's responsibility to "take on" the negative paddler. Those who gossip need to be challenged.

When you listen to gossip and negative expression and remain quiet it is considered "agreement". Be courageous enough to take a stand.

THE MORAL OF THE CANOE THEORY IS...

If you're going to be in the canoe then be in the canoe.

Support the direction, the team members, the leadership and the philosophy of the canoe.

If you cannot support the canoe for any reason, then fight for the change you feel is important, if that change is unable to be delivered then have the integrity to avoid gossip, negativity or anything that undermines the canoe if you stay.

If you are unable to maintain a positive attitude and paddle with the spirit of complete commitment, then have the integrity to leave the canoe.

Staying in the canoe and undermining its integrity should not be an option. Make the choice…. be happy.

Keep your integrity.

Final Thought...

The Canoe Theory is all about choice!

You have the power of choosing the canoe you want to be involved in.

When you choose to be in a canoe... be in the canoe 100%!

The value of being in the canoe 100% is the win you can create for yourself and the canoe.

We've all seen winning teams, and the majority of those teams talk about achieving through the efforts of a group of committed individuals.

Once you've made the commitment, take on a new dimension of responsibility, be a contributor in a way that supports both the organizations success and your own success.

One person can make a difference, and you don't need to own the company to be that one person.

In some cases it is that one individual that stands for positive change that makes a significant difference to a department, to a team or to the entire company.

Leadership is not about a title; it's about a mindset.

There is a motivational plaque that says "We make a Difference ... if we choose!" Next to that statement is a story...

One day a man was walking along the beach when he noticed a figure in the distance.

As he got closer, he realized the figure was that of a boy picking something up and gently throwing it into the ocean.

Approaching the boy, he asked, "What are you doing?"

The youth replied, "throwing a starfish into the ocean. The sun is up and the tide is going out. If I don't throw them back, they'll die."

"Son", the man said, "don't you realize there are miles and miles of beach and hundreds of starfish? You can't possibly make a difference!"

After listening politely, the boy bent down, picked up another starfish, and threw it into the surf.

Then, smiling at the man, he said, "I made a difference for that one."

Adapted from "The Star Thrower" by Loren Eiseley

We all make a difference, one way or another.

What about you and the canoe you are in?

Are you just riding in the canoe or are you contributing?

Are you vested in the direction of the canoe or you just taking up a seat?

One person can make a difference, it takes only small contributions to make big strides.

Ideas To Keep Your Team Paddling...

- These are some outrageous ways to keep The Canoe Theory moving!

- Cut a canoe length- wise and mount it on the office wall. Or for those whose offices allow room, hang a whole canoe from the ceiling.

- Create a team paddle with an inscription "Top Paddler" that rotates quarterly.

- Take a photo of teams/dcpartments paddling.

- Recognize the "Best Paddlers" monthly.

- Designate "The Best Paddler" award annually.

- Fix or lean paddles in each department against the wall.

- Etch The Canoe Theory on a plaque.

- Send "edible" canoes to customers and business partners.

- Integrate The Canoe Theory in your Policy & Procedure manuals.

- Focus on one Canoe Theory tenet per month.

- Print a Canoe Theory tenet on t-shirts and hand them out.

Keep The Canoe Theory alive by referencing it daily. It's an effective way to communicate... it can be the new culture of your organization.

Tell us what you've done to integrate the Canoe Theory into your organization. Let us know how we can support you in growing your canoe!

Email us at <u>canoetheory@profitech.com</u>

For additional information on
Leadership Coaching or Performance Based Strategies
contact Profit Techniques, Inc. at
800-98Profit or 800-987-7634
or visit our web site at www.profitech.com

ABOUT THE AUTHORS...

David R. Hibbard
Sales Training and Leadership Development

David credits himself as a street-smart type, whose true abilities come from working the street more than the desk.

Raised in Chicago and educated at Loyola University, his corporate career began with Proctor & Gamble where the formal side of his background developed.

It didn't take long for him to realize that his talent was drawn to the aggressiveness of the streets and the challenges of high commission selling and managing.

Prior to co-founding Profit Techniques, Dave spent 15 years in the highly competitive, full-commission industry of Commercial Real Estate.

He was the #1 rookie and broker and the #1 sales trainer nation-wide for the Grubb & Ellis Company.

After success brokering, Dave moved to Sr. Vice President where he acquired one of the lowest producing field operations in the Grubb & Ellis chain.

Four years later he was on top again producing one of the most profitable and respected brokerage operations in the Grubb & Ellis organization, by implementing the 7 tenets of the Canoe Theory.

Today, Dave is recognized as one of the most aggressive and extreme sales trainers in the country.

His tactics are uncommon to the standard selling world... the end result produces high volume and high margin strategies for individuals and companies alike.

His ability to instruct sales personnel is unparalleled. He has produced extraordinary sales results for Fortune 500 companies & individuals throughout the U.S. and has defined new high impact paradigms for sales leadership.

Currently, David is a co-principal of Profit Techniques, Inc. in Southern California.

Profit Techniques is a Sales Resource Center.

Marhnelle S. Hibbard
Leadership Development, Sales Training, and Behavioral Specialist.

Marhnelle is a highly regarded and certified strategist advising Fortune 500 and entrepreneurial organizations in the areas of…

> *Leadership Coaching*
> *Executive Strategies*
> *Team Innovation & Problem Solving*
> *Conflict Resolution*
> *Corporate Internal Relationships*
> *Listening and Communication*
> *Organizational Diversity*
> *Behavioral Assessments*
> *Sales Productivity*
> *Time Mastery*

Through her wide variety of capabilities, Marhnelle provides organizations with honest feedback creating greater productivity and profitability for her clients.

Her ability to bring *positive change* to organizations is exceptional.

She is a passionate, high energy, results-driven individual with the ability to comprehend complex corporate issues and provide exceptional working strategies.

Prior to co-founding Profit Techniques, Marhnelle completed 15 years in the Commercial Real Estate Development Industry.

Currently, Marhnelle is a co-partner of Profit Techniques in Southern California.

She and her partner have been providing high impact sales & leadership solutions for a multitude of domestic and international corporations such as:

> *The Irvine Company*
> *Toshiba America*
> *Apple Computer*
> *Gateway Computer*
> *Herman Miller*
> *Quest Software*
> *Steelcase*
> *Shaw Industries*
> *Dupont*

Jack W. Stockman, PH.D.

Dr. Stockman has been a Professor of Human Resources at CSUS since 1970, teaching a variety of courses focusing upon the "people" dimension of organizations.

For the past decade he has taught "The Management of Contemporary Organizations" (OBE 150) through distance learning.

He brings a wealth of experience to the workplace though his many consultation projects with private, public, and non-profit clients.

Dr. Stockman has taught in England, France, and has consulted in Russia, Latvia, and Turkmenistan of the former Soviet Union.

In the fall of 2000, he was invited to China to consult with government and employee representatives on ESOP's and employee ownership.

He is a sought-out trainer, speaker, and management consultant in strategy development, change management and all aspects of human concerns in organizations.

He has served on many non-profit Boards including The Child Abuse Prevention, Community Service Planning Council, Girl Scout Council of Greater Sacramento, and Travelers Aid. He is also an active member of The Rotary Club of Sacramento.

Dr. Stockman earned his BA in Psychology and MS in Management from Southern Illinois University, Carbondale.

He completed Doctoral studies in Organization Theory and Industrial Relations at the University of Washington, Seattle in 1969.

Currently, Dr. Stockman is principal consultant in Stockman and Associates, an organization focusing on strategic and human resource issues in private, public, and non-profit organizations worldwide.

THE CANOE'S RESOURCE LIBRARY...

Every canoe needs a collection of resources on board to assist in the continuous improvement of all dimensions of the effectiveness and efficiency of the organization as well as the growth and development (life-long learning) of each individual team member.

Preferably, these resources will be placed in the front of the canoe so that they may be considered before the white-water rapids are encountered.

Resources include books, trade publications, activities and many other forms of creative tools.

The library is changed frequently; jettisoning old and/or well understood concepts resources to be replaced with new ideas and strategies.

The following resources are but a start, each canoe should build its own Library.

1. *Neat Publications*

2. *Books of Interest for the Canoe (See List)*

Suggested Publications

FastCompany
(www.fastcompany.com)

The Futurist
(www.Wfs.org)

Harvard Business Review
(www.hbsp.harvard.edu)

Red Herring
(www.redherring.com)

Wired
(www.wiredmag.com)

SUGGESTED READINGS

The Boundaryless Organization
Ashkenas, Ron, et. al.
San Francisco: Jossey-Bass Publishers, 1995

Lightning in a Bottle: Proven Lessons for Leading Change
Baum, David
Chicago: Dearborn, a Kaplan Professional Company, 2000

Leaders: Strategies for Taking Charge
Bennis, Warren and Burt Nanus
New York: Harper Business, 2nd Ed., 1997

Why Leaders Can't Lead: The Unconscious Conspiracy Continues
Bennis, Warren
San Francisco: Jossey-Bass Publishers, 1989

The Change Management Handbook
Berger, Lance A. and Martin J. Sikora
New York: McGraw-Hill, 1994

Gung Ho!: Turn On The People In Any Organization
Blanchard, Ken and Sheldon Bowles
New York: William Morrow and Company Inc., 1998

High Five: The Magic of Working Together
Blanchard, Ken and Sheldon Bowles
New York: William Morrow, 2001

The 3 Keys To Empowerment
Blanchard, Ken, Carlos, John P. and Alan Randolph
San Francisco: Berret-Koehler Publishers, Inc. 1999

Raving Fans
Blanchard, Ken and Sheldon Bowles
New York: William Morrow and Company, Inc. 1998

Don't Sweat The Small Stuff...and It's All Small Stuff
Carlson, Richard
New York: Hyperion, 1997

Don't Sweat The Small Stuff at Work
Carlson, Richard
New York: Hyperion, 1998

Don't Sweat The Small Stuff with Your Family
Carlson, Richard
New York: Hyperion, 1998

Don't Sweat The Small Stuff Workbook
Carlson, Richard
New York: Hyperion, 1998

Don't Worry, Make Money
Carlson, Richard
New York: Hyperion, 1997

Management 21C
Chowdhury, Subir
London: Financial Times Prentice Hall, 2000

The New Corporate Cultures. Reading Deal,
Kennedy, Terrence E. and Allan A.
Perseus Books, 1999

Managing In A Time Of Great Change
Drucker, Peter F.
New York: Truman Talley Books/Plume, 1998

Adventures of a Bystander
Drucker, Peter F.
New York: John Wiley & Sons, Inc., 1994

Management Challenges for the 21st Century
Drucker, Peter F.
New York: Harper Business, 1999

On The Profession of Management
Drucker, Peter F.
Boston: Harvard Business School Press, 1998

On Leadership
Gardner, John
New York: The Free Press, 1990

Business @ The Speed Of Thought
Gates, Bill
New York: Warner Books, 1999

Rethinking The Future
Gibson, Rowan
London: Nicholas Brealey Publishing, 1997

Customer Satisfaction Is Worthless, Customer Loyalty Is Priceless
Gitomer, Jeffery
Auston: Bard Press, 1998

The Talent Solution: Aligning Strategy And People To Achieve Extraordinary Results
Gubman, Edward L.
New York: McGraw-Hill, 1998

Leading The Revolution
Hamel, Gary
Boston: TheHarvard Business School Press, 2000

The Age of Paradox
Handy, Charles
Boston: The Harvard Business School Press, 1994

The Age of Unreason
Handy, Charles
Boston: The Harvard Business School Press, 1989

Beyond Certainty
Handy, Charles
Boston: The Harvard Business School Press, 1996

Gods of Management: The Changing Works of Organizations
Handy, Charles
New York: The Oxford University Press, 1995

Understanding Organizations
Handy, Charles
New York: Oxford University Press, 1993

Finding and Keeping Great Employees
Harris, Jim and Joan Brannick
AMACOM, 1999

Six Sigma
Harry, Mikel and Richard Schroeder
New York: Currency Doubleday, 2000

On Managing People
Harvard Business Review
Boston: The Harvard Business School Press, 1999

On Non-Profits
Harvard Business Review
Boston: The Harvard Business School Press, 1999

On Managing Uncertainty
Harvard Business Review
Boston: The Harvard Business School Press, 1999

Leading Beyond The Walls
Hesselbein, Frances, et.al.
San Francisco, Jossey-Bass, 1999

The Service Profit Chain
Heskett, James L. et. al
New York: The Free Press, 1997

Leader To Leader
Hesselbein, Frances, and Paul Cohen, ed The Drucker Foundation
San Francisco: Jossey-Bass, Publishers, 1999

Community of the Future
Hesselbein, Frances, and Paul Cohen, ed The Drucker Foundation
San Francisco: Jossey-Bass, Publishers, 1998

Organization of the Future
Hesselbein, Frances, and Paul Cohen, ed The Drucker Foundation
San Francisco: Jossey-Bass, Publishers, 1997

Leaders of the Future
Hesselbein, Frances, and Paul Cohen, ed The Drucker Foundation
San Francisco: Jossey-Bass, Publishers, 1996

Who Moved My Cheese?
Johnson, Spencer
New York: G.P. Putnam's Sons, 1998

E-Volvet: Succeeding in the Digital Culture of Tomorrow
Kanter, Rosabeth-Moss
Boston: Harvard Business School Press, 2001

The Balanced Scorecard
Kaplan, Robert S. and David P. Norton
Boston: Harvard business School Press, 1996

The Monk and the Riddle
Komisar, Randy
Boston: Harvard Business School Press, 2000

Leading Change
Kotter, John P.
Boston: Harvard Business School Press, 1996

Matsushita Leadership
Kotter, John P.
New York: The Free Press, 1997

The Five Temptations of a CEO
Lencioni, Patrick
San Francisco: Jossey Bass, 1998

Next: The Future Just Happened
Lewis, Michael
New York: W.W. Norton & Company, 2001

Tomorrow's Organizations: Crafting Winning Capabilities in a Dynamic World
Mohrman, Susan Albers, et.al.
San Francisco: Jossey-Bass Publishers, 1998

Global Trends 2005: An Owners Manual For The Next Decade
Mazarr, Michael J.
New York: St. Martin's Press, 1999

Competing By Design
Nadle, David A. and Michael L. Tushman
New York: Oxford University Press, 1997

The Horizontal Organization
Ostroff, Frank
New York: Oxford University Press, 1999

Boundary Crossers: Community Leadership for a Global Age
Pierce, Neal and Curtis Johnson
College Park: The Burns Academy of Leadership Press, 1997

The Human Equation: Building Profits By Putting People First.
Pfeffer, Jeffrey
Boston: Harvard Business School Press, 1998

The New Paradigm in Business
Ray, Michael and Alan Rinzle
New York: G.P. Putnam's Sons, 1993

The Leader's Handbook: Making Things Happen, Getting Things Done
Scholtes, Peter R.
New York: McGraw-Hill, 1998

The Team Handbook: How To Use Teams To Improve Quality
Scholtes, Peter R. et. al.
Madison: Joiner Associates, Inc., 1989

The Dance Of Change
Senge, Peter M.
New York: Currency Doubleday, 1999

The Fifth Discipline: The Art and Practice Of The Learning Organization
Senge, Peter M.
New York: Double Currency, 1990

The Fifth Discipline Fieldbook: Strategies and Tools for Building a Learning Organization
Senge, Peter M., et al.
New York: Doubleday, 1994

The Great Game of Business
Stack, Jack
New York: Currency Doubleday, 1992

Peter Drucker on the Profession of Management
Stone, Nan
Boston: Harvard Business School Press, 1998

Building Wealth: The New Rules for Individuals, Companies, and Nations in a Knowledge-Based Economy
Thurow, Lester C.
New York: Harper Collins Publishers, 1999

In Search of Solutions: 60 Ways to Guide Your Problem-Solving Group
Quinlivan-Hall, David and Peter Renner
Amsterdam: Pfeiffer & Company, 1994

Generations At Work
Zemke, Ron, Claire Raines and Bob Filipczak
New York: AMACOM, 2000